Finger Knitting

the FASTEST, EASIEST, FUNNEST WAY to KNIT!

NO NEEDLES, NO KIDDING!

BY THE EDITORS OF KLUTZ

KLUTZ®

KLUTZ® creates activity books and other great stuff for kids ages 3 to 103. We began our corporate life in 1977 in a garage we shared with a Chevrolet Impala. Although we've outgrown that first office, Klutz galactic headquarters is still staffed entirely by real human beings. For those of you who collect mission statements, here's ours:

• CREATE WONDERFUL THINGS • BE GOOD • HAVE FUN

WRITE US

We would love to hear your comments regarding this or any of our books.

KLUTZ®
568 Broadway, Suite 503
New York, NY 10012
thefolks@klutz.com

Yarn, accessories, and tools manufactured in China. All other parts, Korea. 91

Distributed in the UK by
Scholastic UK Ltd
Westfield Road
Southam, Warwickshire
England CV47 0RA

Distributed in Australia by
Scholastic Australia Ltd
PO Box 579
Gosford, NSW
Australia 2250

Distributed in Canada by
Scholastic Canada Ltd
604 King Street West
Toronto, Ontario
Canada M5V 1E1

Distributed in Hong Kong by
Scholastic Hong Kong Ltd
Suites 2001-2, Top Glory Tower
262 Gloucester Road
Causeway Bay, Hong Kong

ISBN 978-0-545-85845-8
4 1 5 8 5 7 0 8 8 8

CAT EARS,
PAGE 38

table of contents

CIRCLE SCARF,
PAGE 20

SPA SLIPPERS,
PAGE 46

what you get

STITCH HOLDER

This special tool lets you take a break in the middle of knitting.

BEADS & BUTTON

Add these to any project that needs embellishment.

LACING TOOL

Hide loose strands or assemble fancier shapes.

YARN

Each skein of yarn in this book measures 50 yards (46 m)— that's 200 yards (183 m) total!

buying more yarn

YOUR BOOK INCLUDES
200 yards (183 m) of yarn. That's enough to knit two cozy scarves, or 40 little bracelets, or several smallish projects. Once you pick out the project you want to knit, make sure to read the "You'll Need" list before the instructions. It will tell you how many yards of yarn you need to create the project.

After you knit up all the yarn that came with this book, you'll want more. Almost any kind of yarn will work for finger knitting. Really thin or super-thick yarn may look a little different when you finger knit it, but feel free to experiment.

YOU CAN FINGER KNIT WITH ALL KINDS OF THINGS. TRY THESE, IF YOU DARE!

- Ribbons
- Tinsel
- Shoestring licorice
- Recycled T-shirts (page 22)

winding a ball

THE YARN IN THIS BOOK is loosely twisted up in a bundle called a *skein*. Before you start knitting, you will need to wind the yarn into a smooth ball.

1 Untwist the skein and loop it over the top of a chair. If you don't have a chair, ask a friend to hold both hands out and loop the yarn over them. If you're very flexible, try using your feet!

2 Pick up one loose end of the yarn and loop it over your pointer finger and middle finger, winding it around and around. Keep pulling new yarn from the skein.

3 When the yarn on your fingers starts to bulk up, carefully take the bundle off.

4 Wrap the yarn around the middle of the bundle.

> When you finger knit a long chain, store it neatly by winding the finished chain into a ball.

5 Continue wrapping the yarn in random directions around the bundle until you have a nice, round ball.

casting on

WHEN YOU BEGIN A NEW PROJECT, YOU'LL NEED
to set up your loops so they can be finger knit. This setup is
called *casting on*. You only need to do it once for every project
you create.

1 Hold your left hand out with
your palm facing up. Place
the tail of the yarn over your
pointer finger, hanging off
to the left.

2 Weave the long end of the
yarn under your middle
finger, over your ring finger,
and under your pinky.

> Make sure you're
> always weaving with
> the long strand of yarn
> that's attached to the
> ball. Just let that short
> tail hang out by itself.
> You don't need it yet.

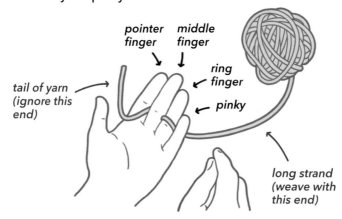

pointer
finger

middle
finger

ring
finger

pinky

tail of yarn
(ignore this
end)

long strand
(weave with
this end)

> Don't wrap the yarn around your
> thumb—just your four fingers.

SAFETY TIP: *Keep the loops
fairly loose, never tight enough
that the yarn might cut off
circulation to your fingers.*

3 Weave the long strand of yarn over your pinky, under your ring finger, over your middle finger, and under your pointer finger.

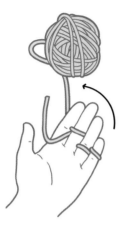

4 Repeat Steps 2-3. You should have two loops on each finger (but nothing on your thumb), with both ends of the yarn hanging off to the left of your hand.

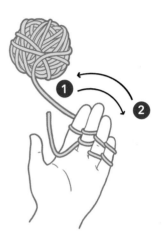

> If you're left-handed and find these instructions confusing, flip to page 18, where you'll find a lefties-only trick for finger knitting.

knitting

NOW THAT YOU'RE ALL SET UP, IT'S TIME FOR the main event: knitting! Starting at your pinky, you'll pick up the loops you made when you cast on.

1 Pinch the bottom pinky loop between the thumb and pointer finger of your right hand. (Leave the top pinky loop where it is.) Lift the loop up and over your pinky, and let it drop to the back.

2 Pull the bottom loop on your ring finger up and over, and then do the same on your middle finger.

3 When you get to your pointer finger, lift the short tail up and over, so it hangs at the back. Now, you should have one loop on each finger.

HELP! I HAVE THREE LOOPS ON MY FINGER!

This happens sometimes if you're knitting really fast. Just pinch the two bottom loops and pull them both over. Your finished piece might have a small bump, but it's not a big deal.

4 To knit your next row, you need two loops on each finger again! So, grab the long end of the yarn (it's hanging between your pointer and middle fingers). Weave it through your fingers, just like you did when you were casting on—weave it over your pointer finger, under your middle finger, over your ring finger, and under your pinky. Then reverse direction, weaving it over your pinky, under your ring finger, over your middle finger and under your pointer finger.

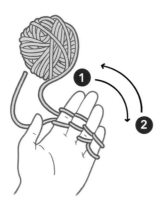

5 You should now have two loops on each finger. Pull the bottom loops over your fingers one at a time, from your pinky to your pointer finger.

6 Repeat Steps 4–5 until your yarn creation is as long as you want it to be. The chain will look a little loose at first. Pull on the end a bit and it will curl up into a nice, even tube.

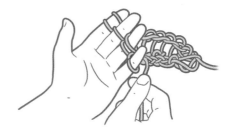

> Always start pulling the loops at your pinky, and move toward your pointer finger.

the RAMBUNCTIOUS SHEEP

A STORY TO HELP REMIND YOU HOW TO KNIT

A FARMER HAS A HERD of sneaky sheep that are always trying to escape their field. One day, the farmer decides to build a fence to pen them in.

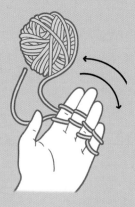

Weave the yarn back and forth between your fingers to make a fence.

AS SOON AS THE FARMER finishes the fence, the sheep jump over it!

Pull the bottom loops up and over your fingers, starting at your pinky and ending at your pointer finger.

REMEMBER THIS STORY if you have trouble keeping track of your finger knitting. The farmer builds a fence. The sheep jump over the fence. The farmer builds a fence. The sheep jump over the fence . . .

HELP! THE YARN IS IN THE WRONG PLACE!

Is your long yarn strand mysteriously floating behind your pinky instead of between your pointer finger and middle finger? Just weave the yarn over your middle finger, and pull the bottom loop on your middle finger up and over. You're back on track!

binding off

WHEN YOU'RE READY TO END THE CHAIN, YOU'LL need to *bind off* the end. This step finishes your loops so that the chain won't unravel.

1 After your last row, you'll have one loop of yarn over each finger. To tie it up nice and neat, start with your pinky as always. Pick up the pinky loop, and move it onto your ring finger.

2 Now you have two loops on your ring finger. Pull the bottom loop up over the top loop, and let it go. Repeat with your middle and pointer fingers until you've got one loop left on your pointer finger, along with the piece of yarn that's still attached to the ball.

3 Cut the yarn from the ball, leaving a tail at least 3 inches (7.5 cm) long.

4 To finish binding off, pull the yarn end through your last loop. Tug on the dangling tails at either end so the chain stretches into a tube. Now show off what you made without any needles at all!

taking a break

SOMETIMES YOU NEED TO PUT YOUR KNITTING down, but you don't want to lose all your hard work. That's when your stitch holder comes to the rescue.

1 Unhook the end of the stitch holder. Hold the pointy end away from yourself.

2 Slip the point of the stitch holder into the first loop of yarn and lift it off your pinky.

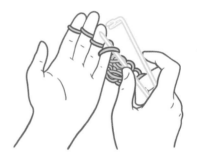

3 Then slip the loops from your ring finger, middle finger, and pointer finger one at a time onto the holder. You'll have four loops total on the stitch holder.

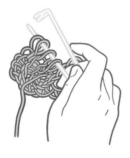

4 Hook the stitch holder back together. Your knitting is ready whenever you are!

If you lose the special stitch holder that comes with this book, you can use a pencil or pen instead. Just make sure that it's in a safe place where it won't get jostled, knocked to the floor, or eaten.

5 To pick up where you left off, unhook the end of the stitch holder. Carefully slide the stitches toward the tip— don't let them fall off. Slip your pointer finger into the first loop.

6 One at a time, slip your middle finger, ring finger, and pinky into the next three loops. You're ready to knit again.

HELP! SOMETHING WENT VERY, VERY WRONG.

You might lose a few rows, but try this fix as a last resort: Take your fingers out of the loops and gently pull on the working yarn (that's the long end, attached to the ball). Keep tugging until you see four new loops pop up, and the working yarn is hanging between the pointer-finger loop and the middle-finger loop. Carefully slip the four loops onto the stitch holder, and then transfer the loops to your fingers.

hiding the tails

WHEN YOU FINISH KNITTING, YOU'LL NOTICE two dangly strands of yarn—one where you started, and one where you finished—called *tails*. Make the knitted chain neat by hiding those loose tails.

1 Thread the tip of the yarn tail through the hole of the lacing tool.

2 Push the tip into the end of the knit chain . . .

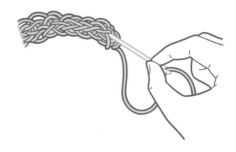

3 . . . and pull it through the chain, out to the side. Try to weave it so the loose end is hidden inside the center of the chain.

4 Remove the lacing tool, and pull on the chain gently. If the tail is sticking out of the side, clip it close to the chain.

lefty technique

SOUTHPAWS (A.K.A. LEFTIES) SHOULD READ this page. If you're left-handed, the previous instructions may feel a little clunky. Here's an easy fix that lets you follow along with all the instructions in this book exactly as written.

1 Hold out your right hand, fingers slightly apart, with your palm facing away from you. Your right hand should look like this:

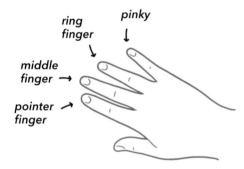

ring finger

pinky ↓

middle finger →

pointer finger ↗

Now, you can follow along with any of the other instructions in the book; just pretend that the left-hand palms in the illustrations are the back of your own right hand.

LEFTY CASTING ON

2 Pinch the short tail of yarn between the thumb and pointer finger of your *right* hand. Weave the long piece of yarn (the piece still attached to the ball) over your pointer finger, under your middle finger, over your ring finger, and under your pinky.

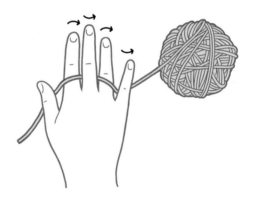

> David Babcock set a world record for knitting the longest scarf while running a marathon. He invented a special type of finger knitting that allows him to knit and run at the same time!

3 Now, reverse direction, weaving the yarn over your pinky, under your ring finger, over your middle finger, and under your pointer finger.

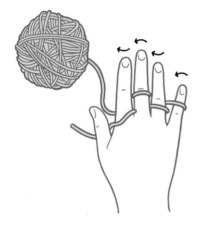

4 Repeat Steps 2-3 so that you have two loops on each finger.

LEFTY KNITTING

5 Starting at your pinky, pick up the bottom loop and pull it over your finger. Repeat for your ring finger, middle finger, and pointer finger.

6 Keep weaving the yarn back and forth between your fingers, and then picking up the bottom loops one at a time. When you're ready to stop, turn to page 13 for how to bind off.

circle scarf

DIFFICULTY LEVEL: ★ ☆ ☆

YOU'LL NEED
* 50 YARDS (46 M) OF YARN

Finger knit one long chain.
Wrap it in a circle. Boom. Done.

1 Knit a *loooong* chain. Seriously, as long as you want (or your yarn will allow). The more yarn you use, the fuller your scarf will be. Hold one end of the finished chain in your hand. Wrap it in a loose circle, big enough to fit over your head. Wrap it over and over, until you can't make another full circle.

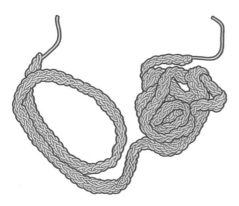

2 Loop the last bit of yarn around the bundle in your hand to secure the circles together. Make sure that both of the loose ends are gathered up so your circle doesn't fall apart.

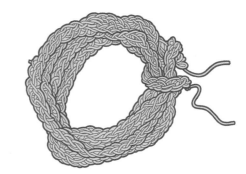

3 Tie the two tails together in a knot. Thread each tail through the lacing tool and hide the ends inside the bundle.

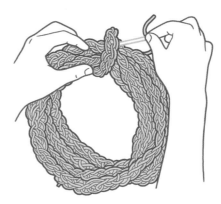

sporty headband

YOU'LL NEED

* 1 T-SHIRT OR 10 YARDS (10 M) OF YARN

DIFFICULTY LEVEL:

Refashion a T-shirt into stretchy, knittable yarn.

SAFETY TIP: Make sure to first get permission from an adult to cut up a T-shirt to make yarn.

1 With scissors, cut a straight line across the T-shirt from armpit to armpit. Discard or recycle the top part of the T-shirt.

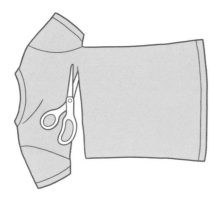

2 Starting at the top edge (where you just cut), carefully cut the T-shirt in a spiral shape, all the way to the bottom. It doesn't have to be perfectly neat, but aim to make the "yarn" about ¾ inch (2 cm) wide. Wind the long strip into a ball.

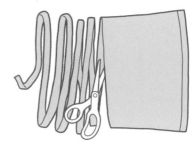

3 Knit a chain long enough to fit around your head comfortably. Stop knitting every once in a while to test it out. Tie the two loose tails together and use the lacing tool to hide the ends.

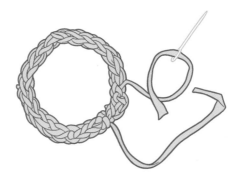

Use leftover scraps from your other projects to make a wild, multicolor fringe.

free-spirit fringe

YOU'LL NEED

* 50 YARDS (46 M) FOR SCARF
* 25 YARDS (23 M) FOR FRINGE

DIFFICULTY LEVEL: ★ ★ ☆

Once you've made a circle scarf, change up the style with boho-chic tassels.

1 Finger knit a chain as long as you want for a scarf. Cut more yarn into strands about 8 inches (20.5 cm) long. (The scarf shown has 100 little strands.)

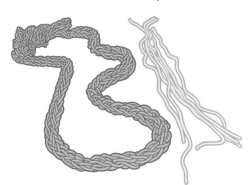

2 Fold a little strand in half, and push the folded end through one loop of the chain.

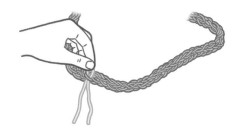

You'll need to buy more yarn— at least 75 yards (69 m)— before you start knitting if you want your scarf and tassels to be all one color.

3 Pull the two loose ends of the little strand through the folded end. Pull tight, and it will close up into a mini tassel. Keep adding little strands in a line around the scarf to make this breezy boho style. Finally, follow the Circle Scarf instructions (page 21) to wrap the long chain into a loop.

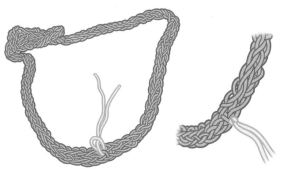

candy stripes

DIFFICULTY LEVEL: ★ ☆ ☆

YOU'LL NEED

* 50 YARDS (46 M) OF PINK
* 50 YARDS (46 M) OF WHITE (OR ANY OTHER COLOR YOU CHOOSE)

Here's the easiest way ever to knit a classic striped scarf.

1 Cut four little strands, about 5 inches long (12.5 cm) from the pink yarn, and four little strands from the white. Set these aside. Knit two chains in pink and two chains in white. The chains should be about the same length (but they don't have to be perfect!). Use the lacing tool to hide the tails. Line up your chains so they alternate pink, white, pink, white.

2 Use one of your little strands from Step 1 to tie all four chains together, about 5 inches from the ends. Tie it tightly in a double knot.

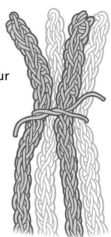

3 Wrap the strand ends around the bundle a few times and tie another double knot to make it sturdy. Use the lacing tool to hide the tails inside the finger-knit chain. Continue along the scarf, tying a strand around the chains every few inches. Stop about 5 inches from the end of the chains, leaving the ends free.

braided ear warmer

YOU'LL NEED

* 20 YARDS (19 M) OF BLUE
* 20 YARDS (19 M) OF GREEN (OR ANY OTHER COLOR YOU CHOOSE)

DIFFICULTY LEVEL: ★ ★ ☆

This fancy four-strand braid only *looks* complicated. The diagonal stripes magically appear as you go.

1 Leaving 10-inch tails (25.5 cm), knit four chains of equal length—two green, two blue. Each chain should be long enough to wrap around your head loosely. Tie the ends of all four chains together in a knot. Place the two green chains on the inside and the blue chains on the outside.

2 Start the four-strand braid: Cross the first (blue) chain over the second (green) chain.

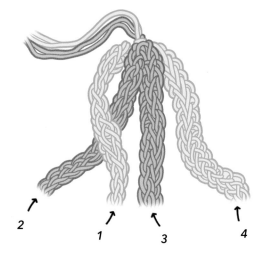

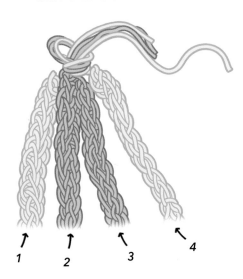

You'll be braiding the four chains, so weigh down the knotted end with something heavy like a book, or have a friend hold it for you.

3 Weave the fourth (blue) chain under the third (green) chain and over the second (blue) chain.

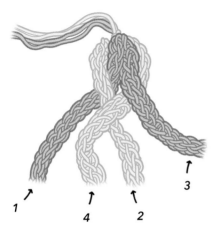

4 Repeat Steps 2-3 until all the chains have been braided together. Tie the end of the braid in a knot. Then braid the four loose tails on both ends, and tie the ends in a knot. To wear it, wrap the ear warmer around your ears and tie the little braided ends together in the back.

You can easily make a matching scarf by knitting four super-duper-long chains. Braid them together the same way you made the headband.

zigzags

DIFFICULTY LEVEL: ★ ★ ★

Whoa! Finger knit with two contrasting colors at once to create zigs, zags, and pizzazz.

YOU'LL NEED

* 50 YARDS (46 M) OF PINK
* 50 YARDS (46 M) OF BLUE (OR COLORS OF YOUR CHOICE)

1 Cast on and knit your first row with blue yarn. You should now have one loop on each finger.

It helps to place the balls of yarn on a table, where you can switch them back and forth each time you switch colors. This prevents the long strands of yarn from tangling around each other.

2 Using the pink yarn, weave one row of loops back and forth between your fingers. The blue and pink yarn tails should both be hanging out to the left of your hand now.

3 Pinch the bottom (blue) loops, and pull them up over your fingers, starting from your pinky and working toward your pointer finger.

4 On the next row, pick up the working strand of blue yarn, making sure that it wraps around the *outside* of the pink yarn strand that's attached to the ball. Weave one row of loops back and forth, then pull the pink loops over your fingers, from pinky to pointer finger.

5 Continue knitting a chain, alternating between the two colors. To prevent your yarn from tangling, always make sure that the new color wraps around the *outside* of the old color. When you're done, bind off all stitches normally, moving each loop to the next finger and knitting those stitches. Cut the yarns and use the lacing tool to hide the four loose ends.

Feel free to make any of the projects in this book with zigzag stripes instead of solid colors.

SNAKE!!

TURN YOUR ZIGZAG SCARF into a cute snake: Sew two beads onto one end to create eyes. Tie a small piece of yarn to the very last stitch for a little tongue.

TRY MAKING SNAKES WITH any leftover colors from other projects.

button cuff bracelet

YOU'LL NEED
* 4 YARDS (4 M) FOR 1 BRACELET
* 1 BUTTON

DIFFICULTY LEVEL: ★ ☆ ☆

Make 'em, trade 'em, or give 'em away. All you need is a little bit of yarn and a cute button.

1 Knit a short chain, just long enough to fit around your wrist. Thread a button onto one loose tail and slide it as close to the knit chain as possible. Wrap the thread around the button twice to tie a double knot. Tie it once again for a stronger knot.

> Knitted bracelets have a bit of stretch, so one bracelet will fit a range of wrist sizes.

2 Thread each loose tail of yarn onto the lacing tool, and weave them into the knit chain to hide the ends.

3 To wear your bracelet, wrap the chain around your wrist, and push the button through any gap in the knit chain. Ask a friend to help you if it's tricky.

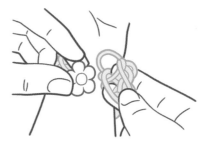

beaded necklace

DIFFICULTY LEVEL: ★ ★ ☆

A little bit of knitting. A whole lot of style.

YOU'LL NEED

* 5 YARDS (5 M) OF YARN
* 10 BEADS

1 String all of the beads onto your yarn. Let them hang out close to the ball of yarn—you won't need them just yet. Leave a 14-inch tail (35.5 cm) hanging from your pointer finger. Cast on, and knit one row. You should have one loop left on each finger.

For a quick refresher, see pages 8–11 to cast on and knit a row.

2 It's time to add a bead! Slide the first bead up your yarn toward your hand. When you wrap the yarn around your pointer finger, adjust the bead so it sits snugly against your pointer finger, as shown. Continue weaving back and forth, and then pull the bottom loops over your fingers one at a time, from your pinky to your pointer finger.

3 Repeat Step 2, sliding one bead up to your pointer finger each time you knit a row, until you are out of beads.

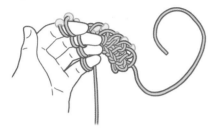

4 Bind off all the stitches until you have one loop remaining on your pointer finger. Leaving a 14-inch tail, cut your yarn. Thread the end of the tail through the last loop on your pointer finger. Pull the tails tight on either side. Tie the ends in a bow to create a clasp.

Some beads might look a little wonky when you finish the necklace. That's OK! Just scoot the beads down so each one dangles at the bottom of its yarn loop.

Mix and match your own beads to make a multicolored necklace! If you're not using the beads that come with this book, just make sure that the hole is large enough to string onto your yarn.

cat ears

DIFFICULTY LEVEL: ★ ★ ☆

Once you've braided an ear warmer, try adding these too-cute toppers!

YOU'LL NEED
* 20-50 YARDS (19-46 M) OF YARN
* 2 PIPE CLEANERS

1 Bend a pipe cleaner in half to find the center. This will be the pointy top of one ear. Crease the middle and let it spring out into a triangle shape.

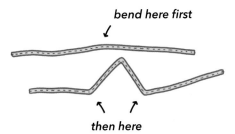

bend here first

then here

2 Knit a short chain, about 10 inches (25.5 cm) long. Tie one end around the base of the pipe cleaner triangle, and then wrap the rest around the triangle, until you reach the other side.

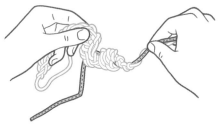

3 Tie off the other tail on the other side of the triangle. Repeat Steps 1–3 to make a second ear.

4 Knit and braid an ear warmer. Follow the instructions for a Sporty Headband (page 22) or a Braided Ear Warmer (page 28). Position the ears where you want them above the headband, and then weave the pipe cleaner ends into the chains to secure them.

lazy daisy

DIFFICULTY LEVEL:

These blooms look fresh, even in the middle of winter.

YOU'LL NEED
* 10 YARDS (10 M) FOR 1 DAISY

1 Knit a medium-length chain, about 20 inches (51cm) long. Thread one loose tail through your lacing tool.

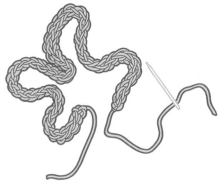

2 Fold the end of the chain into a petal shape about 2 inches (5 cm) long, and push the lacing tool through the base. Pull the lacing tool tightly to create the first petal.

3 Fold the chain to create a second petal shape directly next to the first petal. Make sure they are about the same size. Push the lacing tool through the new petal.

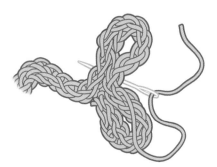

4 Repeat folding the chain and lacing each petal together all the way around. You should have five or six petals total. For extra security, you can weave the tail through all the petals once more after the daisy shape is complete.

5 Use the lacing tool to hide the tails on the back of the daisy.

Daisies look cute on almost anything! Sew one to a headband or a scarf (page 42).

To make this fancy flower, stack daisies of different sizes and sew them through the center with a piece of yarn. Try sewing a bead or button to the center.

blossom scarf

DIFFICULTY LEVEL: ★ ★ ☆

Pick your two best Lazy Daisies to embellish a delicate braid.

YOU'LL NEED
* 50 YARDS (46 M) FOR BRAID
* 20 YARDS (37 M) FOR FLOWERS

1 Snip two strands of green yarn about 4 inches (10 cm) long and set them aside. With the rest of the green yarn, knit three chains, each about 30 inches (76 cm) long, or long enough make a little scarf. Use the lacing tool to hide the tails. Tie one of the short strands of green yarn (shown here in purple so you can see it) around the bundle of three chains, about 4 inches from one end.

2 Wrap the short strand of yarn around a few more times, and then tie a double knot. Use your lacing tool to hide the loose ends.

3 Braid the three strands by crossing the right chain over the middle chain; then cross the left chain over the middle chain. Repeat until the entire length is braided. Tie the other end as you did in Steps 1 and 2.

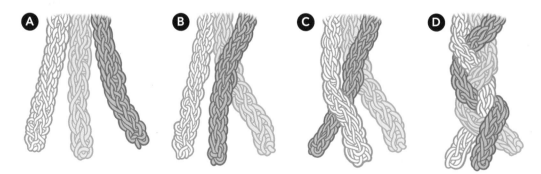

4 With the pink yarn, make two Lazy Daisies (page 40), keeping the tails long. Add one daisy to each end of the braid, where you tied the ends together. Use the tails to tie each daisy around the braid, and hide any loose tails.

bouquet chain

YOU'LL NEED
* 200 YARDS (183 M) TOTAL

· ·

DIFFICULTY LEVEL: ★ ★ ★

Hang this floral arrangement in your room, or wear it as an over-the-top statement scarf.

1 Make a big pile of Lazy Daisies (page 40)—about 15-20 flowers will do the trick. Cut a long strand of yarn about 40 inches (102 cm) and thread it onto the lacing tool.

2 Lay one of the daisies flat on a table. Insert the lacing tool through the tip of a petal and out through the opposite side.

3 Leave a little tail of yarn where you started, and continue to string each flower onto the strand of yarn. For extra security, turn the lacing tool around when you're done and sew back in the opposite direction. Hide the tails in the flowers on each end.

spa slippers

DIFFICULTY LEVEL: ★ ★ ☆

Warm up your beach-bum sandals with yarn for a perfect at-home spa day.

1 Cast on and knit your first row. When you have only one loop on each finger, carefully lift the pointer-finger loop off your finger.

2 Wrap the loop under your flip-flop strap (at the base), and place the loop back on your pointer finger.

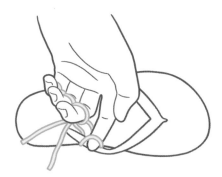

You can cover tons of stuff with finger knitting! Headphones, hair ties, pencils, mug handles, Hula-Hoops, drumsticks, chopsticks, regular ol' sticks, straws, skinny belts, tote bag straps, slingshots, magic wands, jump ropes . . .

3 Weave more yarn back and forth between your fingers, and pull the bottom loops over your fingers, starting at your pinky and ending at your pointer finger.

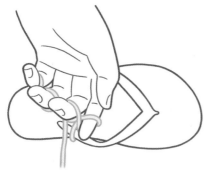

When you're done, there should be a loop of yarn locked around the strap.

4 Repeat Steps 2–3. Continue knitting along the strap, wrapping the pointer finger loop around the flip-flop strap on each row. Bind off the stitches. Then use the lacing tool to wrap each tail around the flip-flop strap and hide the tails.

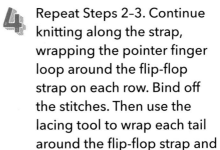

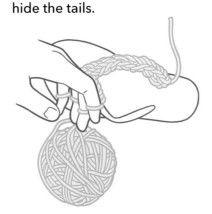

boot toppers

DIFFICULTY LEVEL: ★ ★ ★

Keep that chilly wind from sneaking into your boots. Wear them over stockings or even jeans!

1 Knit a chain long enough to wrap around the widest part of your calf, but *do not bind off*. Keeping the yarn on your fingers, pick up two loops side-by-side from the very first row (near the dangling tail), and place that set of loops on your pinky. It's not really important which loops you choose, but make sure they're close to the dangling tail.

look for this "V" shape

2 Weave the yarn back and forth between your fingers (including your pinky), as if to knit. You will have four loops on your pinky. All your other fingers will have two loops as usual.

3 Pick up the *three* bottom loops from your pinky, and pull them *all* up and over your finger. Then knit the rest of your fingers as usual.

4 Before you weave more yarn, pick up another set of loops from the chain you already knit. Make sure that the loops you pick up are right next to the last ones you grabbed. Repeat Step 3, pulling the bottom *three* loops from your pinky up and over your finger, and then knitting the rest of your fingers normally.

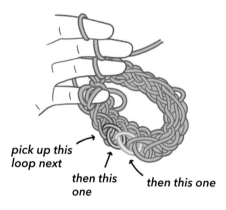

pick up this loop next

then this one

then this one

To turn these toppers into mitts, make the chain in Step 1 big enough to wrap around the palm of your hand. Continue following Steps 2–5. To wear them as fingerless mitts, slip the tube over your hand and wrist. Poke your thumb through a gap in the knitting to create a thumbhole.

5 Repeat Step 4, knitting all the way around the circle to make a tube. When your tube is long enough, bind off the four stitches on your fingers. Use the lacing tool to weave in the ends. Then make a second topper so your other leg doesn't feel left out in the cold.

If you look closely and straighten out your chain, you'll see that all of your stitches line up row by row. To keep the tube neat, pick up your stitches all in a straight line, and don't skip any.

If your tube is too loose, grab the two ends and pull. You'll stretch it out, making a skinnier (and taller) topper.

spiral hat

DIFFICULTY LEVEL: ★ ★ ★

No one will ever believe you made this with your own two hands—literally.

YOU'LL NEED

* 75 YARDS (69 M) OF YARN (DEPENDING ON THE SIZE OF YOUR HEAD, YOU MAY NOT USE ALL OF IT)

1 Knit a chain long enough to wrap around your head loosely, but *do not bind off*. Pick up two loops from your very first row (where the dangling tail is) and place it on your pinky. Look for the two loops that form a horizontal "V" shape along the edge of the chain.

2 Keeping the extra two loops on your pinky, weave the yarn back and forth as usual between your fingers, including your pinky. You should have four loops on your pinky. All your other fingers will have two loops as usual.

This project is a little tricky at first, so practice by knitting a Boot Topper (page 48), and then wind the yarn back into a ball to reuse it for this hat. Depending on the size of your head, a hat can use a lot of yarn, so you may want to buy more yarn before you begin.

3 Pull the bottom *three* loops from your pinky up and over. Then knit the rest of your fingers as usual.

4 Before you weave more yarn through your fingers for the next row, use your pinky to pick up another stitch from the chain below. To keep the spiral neat, pick up your stitches all in a straight line and don't skip any.

5 Knit all the way around the circle, picking up a stitch (two loops) with your pinky on every row. Knit about six or seven circles so you have a short tube.

6 Now it's time to *decrease* the crown of the hat. (In knitting lingo, that means closing up the top so you can wear it!) Instead of picking up every stitch from the chain below, pick up every *other* stitch.

7 Keep knitting around and around. The tube will start to get smaller.

8 When you can't knit any more because the spiral is closed at the top of the hat, bind off the stitches. Use the lacing tool to weave in the tails. Weave the tail at the top a few times in different directions to make sure it's secure.

Your hat might look pointy when it's finished. Just stretch the sides gently and it will even out.

credits

YARN DETANGLER: Caitlin Harpin

TOTALLY TWISTED: Katie Benezra

TECH ARTIST: Kyle Hilton

PHOTOGRAPHERS: Gale Zucker and Michael Frost

SLIGHTLY LOOPY: Owen Keating

KNITTY GRITTY: Linda Olbourne

HIP KNITSTERS: Sara Katz, Sarah Rosenthal, and Karima Sundarji

WOOLY WONDERS: Netta Rabin and Hannah Rogge

KITTEN WRANGLER: Barrie Zipkin

POM-POM SHAKER: Stacy Lellos

WARM THANKS TO OUR MODELS: Amalia, Emma, Isabel, Jordan, Ryan, and Max

Here are more Klutz books we think your kids will like.

Hey Parents...
Want to see SOMETHING
REALLY KLUTZY?

 Klutz Books

 Klutz Books

 Klutz

 @KlutzBooks

KLUTZ.COM

Visit us to find a nearby retailer.

e-mail us at thefolks@klutz.com or give us a call at 1-800-737-4123

We'd love to hear from you.